Peter J.C. Skelton and Nils Huxtable

First published in the United Kingdom in 1982 by
Jane's Publishing Company Limited
238 City Road, London EC1V 2PU

ISBN 0 7106 0223 5

Printed by
Toppan Printing Co. (s) Pte Ltd
38 Liu Fang Road, Jurong, Singapore 2262

Front cover photo: *Peter J.C. Skelton*
Rear cover photo: *Peter Millar*
This page: *Nils Huxtable*

INTRODUCTION

The date of 11 August 1968 is recalled with sadness by British steam enthusiasts for it witnessed the infamous 'Fifteen Guinea Special' commemorating the end of steam traction on British Railways. After this day the future looked bleak indeed. To compound the sense of loss a ban was imposed by BR on the use of steam locomotives over its tracks, the one exception being Gresley A3 Pacific *Flying Scotsman*. Even this fine machine, although under contract to run until 1971, left British shores for a tour of North America in 1969.

Those who endured the worst up to that fateful day in August were left with some bitter memories. The last months of steam operation had been far from glorious. Bereft of name and number plates the dwindling numbers of ex-LMS and BR Standard engines presented a sorry sight. Even the strongest advocates of progress must have questioned the headlong abandonment of steam on seeing row upon row of recently overhauled and perfectly serviceable locomotives with their piston rods cut through.

During the years that immediately followed the preservation society lines helped compensate the loss of the real thing. On the Severn Valley Railway, the Keighley and Worth Valley or the Bluebell it was possible on a summer afternoon to pretend the 'Beeching Plan' and the great purge of steam had never occurred. But the Kings, Merchant Navies, Duchesses and A4s were gone from the main lines and BR's truncated network would never be the same without them.

All that changed in October 1971 when *King George V* unexpectedly burst into the autumn sunshine with its train of 'Cider Pullmans'. In a dramatic reversal of its ban, BR resolved to allow lovers of steam to enjoy once again the spectacle and experience of main line steam in action.

This changed attitude gave many preservation groups a strong incentive to restore their locomotives to main line running standards. At the same time enthusiast and public affection for the steam era ensured that further sections of the nation's railway heritage were saved as railway preservation flourished. One essential and unique component in the development of this movement was Barry. Without the fortuitous lines of rusting locomotive hulks at Dai Woodham's scrapyard, many preservation schemes might have foundered for want of adequate motive power and the main line steam scene in the 1980s would have been very much the poorer. It is all too easy to forget when glancing at the superbly restored Jubilee 4-6-0 No 5690 *Leander* that this engine once stood in that same Barry scrap line weathered by corrosive sea breezes, and it is no discredit to the dedicated teams behind such schemes to acknowledge also the tolerance and understanding of the charismatic South Wales scrap dealer.

A decade of main line steam running brought back some of the best examples of British locomotive practice and gave appetising glimpses of steam as it was in its colourful heyday. It also brought a more mature approach to the complex process of managing and marketing steam-hauled excursions, culminating in the formation of the Steam Locomotive Operators Association and the sponsorship of summertime steam specials by BR.

In the pages which follow are portrayed many of the finest products of British railway preservation and restoration, ranging from locomotives of the pre-nationalisation 'Big Four' through to BR Standard designs, industrials in use on society lines and, briefly, broad gauge gems from Ireland. The final section of the book is devoted appropriately to narrow gauge steam and includes views of the historic lines which pioneered working railway preservation in the United Kingdom.

As we hope these pictures demonstrate, the British steam revival is very much in progress for those who care to seek it out.

Acknowledgements

We wish to convey our grateful thanks to all who contributed valuable colour transparencies for reproduction in this book.

Our thanks extend also to Stewart Blencowe, Ken Harris and Danuta Skelton for their valued assistance.

Peter J.C.Skelton
Nils Huxtable

February 1982

On duty
GWR 0-4-2T No 1450 reverses out of Buckfastleigh depot, passing 0-6-0PT No 1638 before coupling onto chocolate and cream coaching stock for the picturesque run alongside the River Dart to Totnes, on a glorious summer day on the Dart Valley Railway on 15 July, 1981. *(Peter J.C.Skelton)*
Hasselblad 500CM, 80mm   *Ektachrome 64*   *f5.6, 1/250*

Before the storm
As rainclouds roll in, the
Severn Valley Railway's
Churchward 2-8-0 No 2857
gives the illusion of
working a heavy freight as
it enters the last of the
sunshine at Bewdley from
Foley Park during a filming
sequence for the BBC's
God's Wonderful Railway
on 19 July, 1980.
(Peter J.C.Skelton)
Contax RTS, 50mm
Kodachrome K25
f2, 1/500

Severn pastoral
One of Severn Valley Railway's pioneer engines, Collett 0-6-0 No 3205, back at work after being out of service for seven years, complements the Shropshire landscape with a Bridgnorth-Bewdley train, composed entirely of GW chocolate and cream coaches on 28 June, 1981. *(Nils Huxtable)*
Pentax K1000, 50mm   Kodachrome K64

Poetry in motion
This prize winning panned view of No 4079 *Pendennis Castle* shows the stylish Collett design to full advantage as the immaculate engine heads a private excursion chartered by Mr W.McAlpine between Hereford and Shrewsbury on a lovely spring day in April, 1974. No 4079 is still mourned by GW enthusiasts since its transportation to Australia. *(Hugh Ballantyne)*

Leica M3, 50mm   *Kodachrome K25*   *f8, 1/60*

Glorious Devon
The Great Western Railway's long association with Devonshire seaside resorts is typified in this view of Prairie tank No 4555 passing a small cove between Goodrington and Broadsands on 17 July, 1981 returning empty stock to Churston after a successful day on the Torbay Steam Railway. *(Peter J.C. Skelton Hasselblad 500CM, 80mm Ektachrome 64   f4, 1/500*

Low tide
Early days of the Torbay Steam Railway following the transition period from British Rail to private ownership. Collett Prairie No 4588 is reflected in the waters of the Dart estuary as it takes the first train of the morning out of Kingswear in May 1973.
(Nils Huxtable)
Pentax, 50mm   *Kodachrome K64*

Last light
The rapidly setting sun tints the pure steam exhaust from the Severn Valley Railway's GWR 4-6-0 No 4930 *Hagley Hall* and LMS 4-6-0 No 5000 (on loan from the NRM) as they approach Bayston Hill on the climb out of Shrewsbury with the return 'Inter-City' charter train between Hereford and Chester on 22 September, 1979. The two mixed traffic locomotives were painstakingly restored by SVR's Bridgnorth team whose final paint touches were applied to *Hagley Hall* just 48 hours previously, ensuring it made its main line debut in resplendent condition. *(Peter J.C.Skelton)*

Hasselblad 500CM, 80mm   Ektachrome pro 200   f2.8, 1/500

Fine finish
The sun finally breaks through the clouds at Ponthir as No 4930 *Hagley Hall* with its burnished brass and polished paintwork glistening hurries the 'Welsh Marches Express' away from Newport on 14 March, 1981. *(Nils Huxtable)*
Pentax K1000 135mm   *Kodachrome K64*

Sunset
The setting sun casts a golden glow over 'The Sunset' charter train hauled by GWR No 5051 *Drysllwyn Castle* complete with the Great Western Society's vintage chocolate and cream set. The classic combination powers up the 1:251 gradient at Fenny Compton, on the return trip to Didcot from Stratford upon Avon on 26 January, 1980. (Dr W.A.Sharman)

Mamiya 645   Ektachrome pro 64   f2.8, 1/125

White magic
Nature's magnificence enhances the pictorial splendour of Severn Valley Railway GWR 2-6-2T No 5164 accelerating an eight coach 'Santa Steam' train alongside Northwood Lane through spectacular winter snow between Arley and Bewdley on 12 December, 1981. *(Peter J.C.Skelton)*
Hasselblad 500CM, 80mm   Agfachrome pro R100S   f5.6/8, 1/500

Over the arches
Churchward heavy 2-8-0T No 5239, although formerly assigned to the South Wales coalfields, does not look out of place on a passenger train. Seen here crossing Maypool viaduct on 6 July, 1979, the big goods locomotive heads the last train of the day from Kingswear to Paignton. *(Nils Huxtable)*
Pentax K1000 135mm   Kodachrome K64

First run
No 6998 *Burton Agnes Hall* had already become a familiar sight by the date of this picture. Here, however, she is coupled to an 'unmodified' member of the class, No 5900 *Hinderton Hall*, on its first main line assignment since restoration. The two gleaming 4-6-0s pass Cropredy just north of Banbury, with a Great Western Society special on 15 May, 1976. *(Peter J.C. Skelton)*
Canon FTb, 50mm   Kodachrome K64   f4, 1/250

Royal Sovereign
An important part of preservation is the restoration of coaches from various companies and origins. To celebrate 100 years of on-train catering, the National Railway Museum at York assembled nine historic dining cars to form 'The Centenary Express' which made special appearances out on the main line over a two week period. GWR 4-6-0 No 6000 *King George V*, immaculately turned out by courtesy of Messrs Bulmers, heads the Travellers' Fare 'Centenary Express' out of Hereford station on 15 September, 1979 with the working up to Shrewsbury and back. *(Peter J.C.Skelton)*
Hasselblad 500CM, 80mm
Ektachrome pro 64   f4, 1/500

Castle run
No 7029 *Clun Castle* climbs the west side of Hatton bank at Shrewley on 3 April, 1977 with the 'Midland Wightsman', which made visits to both the Birmingham Railway Museum and Warwick Castle. This locomotive headed no fewer than three titled trains during the same day, 'The Kingmaker', 'Midland Wightsman' and 'The Bookman'.
No 7029 was the last 'Castle' in service and made a number of special runs, including one as far north as Carlisle, before being temporarily retired in 1967. *(Peter J.C.Skelton)*
Canon FTb, 50mm   Kodachrome K64
f4, 1/500

Great Western glory

It is hay baling time as No 7808 *Cookham Manor* and No 6998 *Burton Agnes Hall* make the return journey from Hereford to Didcot shortly after leaving Ledbury tunnel with the Great Western Society vintage train on 14 June, 1975. *(Peter J.C.Skelton)*

Canon FTb, 50mm   *Kodachrome K64*   *f4, 1/500*

Backlit

After many years on the Cambrian and South Devon banks, No 7812 *Erlestoke Manor* finds itself suited to the Severn Valley Railway, where it is seen leaving Bewdley with a train for Bridgnorth on 13 September, 1980. For a small class the *Manors* are well represented with nine extant survivors, although to date only No 7812 has been restored in authentic BR lined green livery. *(Stewart Blencowe)*

Mamiya DSX1000, 50mm   *Kodachrome K64*   *f4, 1/500*

Dukedog
At the time of its withdrawal in 1960 from Machynlleth depot after service on the Cambrian Coast line, former GWR 4-4-0 No 9017 was the last double framed locomotive in service. It has since been restored on the Bluebell Railway to Great Western green as No 3217 *Earl of Berkeley*, and is pictured approaching Freshfield Halt on a typical Sussex summer day. *(Michael Squire)*

Pentax SV, 50mm   Kodachrome K11   f4, 1/250

GI Joes
Without the tireless efforts and enthusiasm of active members on preserved lines, impressive combinations such as this one of US-built Nos 72 'Little Jim' and 5820 'Big Jim', pictured shortly after leaving Mytholmes tunnel, would not have been possible. The 2-8-0 locomotive No 5820 was designed to the British loading gauge and was purchased and transported from Poland to work trains on the Keighley & Worth Valley Railway. (*Laurie Manns*)
Bronica S2A, 75mm
Ektachrome pro 64   *f4, 1/500*

Generations apart

The stately Adams radial tank No 488 of 1882 joins forces with the purely functional wartime US Army dock shunter No 30064 to work an enthusiasts' weekend train in September 1976. The duo are seen approaching Freshfield Halt. *(Peter J.C.Skelton)*

Canon FTb, 50mm   Kodachrome K64   f2.8/4, 1/500

Peaceful valley
The ruggedly constructed SR 4-6-0 S15 No 841 *Greene King* fails to disturb the tranquil peace of the countryside as it heads towards Pickering along the beautiful

Esk Valley with a train from Grosmont on the North Yorkshire Moors Railway in May, 1980. (*John Hunt*)

Pentax, 50mm   Kodachrome K25

Smoke screen
Southern Railway malachite green No 850 *Lord Nelson* takes its first assault over the Settle and Carlisle line in its stride as it storms around the curve into Dent station on 31 July, 1980 after topping Ais Gill Summit with a southbound 'Cumbrian Mountain Express'. *(Peter J.C. Skelton)*
Hasselblad 500CM, 80mm   Ektachrome 64   f4, 1/500

Winter's glint
A truly dramatic picture is created by the bleak landscape, low winter sun, dark clouds and windswept steam as No 850 *Lord Nelson* restarts the 'Cumbrian Mountain Express' away from a photo stop at Garsdale on 24 January, 1981 and crosses Dandry Mire Viaduct. (*Andrew Madden*)
Pentax K1000, 50mm   Kodachrome K64   *f5.6, 1/250*

Schools return

Good news in 1981 for Southern enthusiasts was the return to steam of No 928 *Stowe*, one of Maunsell's classic engines. The Schools locomotives were Britain's last and most powerful 4-4-0 design. No 928 is pictured on 14 June, 1981 surrounded by summer's greenery as it draws towards Freshfield Halt with complementary Southern stock. *(Hugh Ballantyne)*

Leica M4-2, 50mm   Kodachrome K25   f2-8, 1/500

Freshfield
Worth more than a passing glance, Wainwright SECR 0-4-4T No 263 arouses the
interest of a bovine bystander as it ascends Freshfield bank on a crisp November day

in 1977. *(Martin Wilkins)*
Canon EF, 50mm   Kodachrome K25   f2.8/4, 1/250

Vintage Bluebell
The first preserved standard
gauge branch line in the
country has lost none of its
charm after more than two
successful decades. Diminu
class P 0-6-0T No 323 *Blue*
herself recalls the early day
she celebrates the 20th
Anniversary of the line's fir
steam hauled passenger trai
on 3 August, 1980. *(Alan
J.Powick)*
Rolleiflex 2.8E, 80mm.
Ektachrome 64   f4, 1/.

Wainwright elegance
The beautifully restored South Eastern & Chatham Railway Class C 0-6-0 No 592 drifts casually towards Freshfield Halt on 12 October, 1975 after topping the bank with a Sheffield Park to Horsted Keynes train on the Bluebell Railway. *(Michael Squire)*

Canon EX, 50mm   Kodachrome K25   f2.8/4, 1/250

Last train
Another member of the Bluebell's varied loco stud, Maunsell class U No 1618, built at Brighton in October 1928, is seen here once again working back in its home country, catching the late afternoon sunlight on 14 June, 1981 with the last northbound train of the day from Sheffield Park about a mile from Horsted Keynes.
(Hugh Ballantyne)

Leica M4-2, 50mm   Kodachrome K25   f2/2.8, 1/500

Island greenery
Travelling through summer's lush greenery on the tranquil Isle of Wight Steam Railway on 9 July, 1981 is newly restored LBSCR class A1X 0-6-0T No W8 *Freshwater*, seen between Haven Street and Wooton. *(Graham Wignall) Mamiya 645, 80mm   Ektachrome 64*

Filling the picture

A welcome addition to the growing list of preserved lines is the Mid-Hants. No 34016 *Bodmin*, the first rebuilt West Country to make a comeback, bursts out of the cutting at Alresford in October, 1979. This locomotive is the first of four Bulleid Pacifics on the 'Watercress Line' to be made serviceable, so promising much premier power for the future. *(Graham Wignall)*

Canon A1, 50mm   Agfa CT18

Southern flashback

The Southern's heyday is recalled in this scene of No 21C123 *Blackmore Vale*, restored to latter day SR livery complete with a set of Southern coaches, passing under an occupation bridge near Freshfield Halt in September, 1976, just as the leaves indicate autumn's approach. *(Peter J.C.Skelton)*
Canon FTb, 50mm   Kodachrome K64   f2.8, 1/500

Golden Arrow
Memories of the 'Golden Arrow' passing through Kent's wintry carpet behind one of Bulleid's Pacifics are relived in this view of No 34092 *City of Wells* hauling the

Keighley and Worth Valley Railway Society's special through Bentham on 12 December, 1981, a day of severe winter conditions. *(Michael Whyment)*
Nikon FM   *Agfa CT21*   *f8, 1/250*

Clan Line at Clapham

With characteristic efficiency Merchant Navy class Pacific No 35028 *Clan Line*, the first ex-SR express engine to return to main line running, drifts upgrade from

Clapham with the 'North Yorkshireman' on 4 July, 1979. *(Nils Huxtable)*

Pentax K1000, 50mm   *Kodachrome K64*

Homeward bound

The many exhibitions and open days that followed the Rainhill Exposition had a star attraction when the graceful Midland 'Spinner' was shown to gathering admirers. The beautiful MR 4-2-2 No 673 returned to steam after a lapse of nearly fifty years thanks to the devotion of the Butterley team, and is seen on 15 June, 1980 coupled to LMS 0-6-0 4F No 4027 passing Tapton Junction, Chesterfield after appearing at the Tinsley Open Day. (*L.A.Nixon*)

Nikon F, 85mm   Kodachrome K25

Dignity and impudence
Although only a decade older than the Midland Compound No 1000, LNWR 2-4-0 No 790 *Hardwicke* of 1892 seems a grandfather by comparison. Both engines are hauling a special from York to Carnforth on 24 April, 1976 and catch a short burst of sunlight near Cononley, running along the valley of the River Aire. *(Hugh Ballantyne)*

Leica M3, 90mm   Kodachrome K25   f4 1/125

Crimson Lake

The finest matching combination available to haul main line specials is undoubtedly MR Compound 4-4-0 No 1000 and LMS Jubilee 4-6-0 No 5690 *Leander*. The crimson lake duo catch the imagination as they accelerate away from Leeds and approach Bramhope tunnel with the 'Leander Enterprise' special on 20 October, 1979. *(Peter J.C.Skelton)*

Hasselblad 500CM, 80mm   Ektachrome pro 64   f4, 1/500

Early morning
A crisp sunny morning picks out the white exhaust from Ivatt 2-6-2T No 41241, sporting lined black livery, as it hauls a set of maroon coaches over Mytholmes

viaduct on the Keighley and Worth Valley Railway on 22 March, 1980. *(Peter Millar)*
Mamiya 645   *Ektachrome 64*   *f4, 1/500*

Twenty five below
BR-built Ivatt 2-6-0 No 43106 receives attention at Bewdley on 12 December, 1981 in a desperate attempt to make the locomotive serviceable after minus twenty five degrees of frost. Despite being in steam overnight alongside bonfires, frozen pipes and seized brakes took their time to yield to the morning sun. *(Peter J.C. Skelton)*
Hasselblad 500CM, 80mm   Ektachrome pro 64   f8/11, 1/125

The Pines remembered
Snow on the high ground and a mushroom cloud of smoke and steam show winter has yet to yield as Fowler 0-6-0 '4F' No 43924 hammers towards Oakworth after leaving Damens Loop. The engine which was to have piloted the unavailable

No 34092 *City of Wells* re-enacts the 'Pines Express' single-handed on 22 March, 1980. (*John S. Whiteley*)
Pentax, 85mm   *Kodachrome K25*   *f4 1/250*

Crew training
LMS '4F' No 4027 looks a
picture as it crosses Butterley
reservoir along the causeway
with a rake of maroon coaches
during crew training runs on
the Midland Railway Centre's
line on 20 December, 1980.
(Laurie Manns)
Bronica S2A, 75mm
Ektachrome pro 64
f8, 1/250

Black beauty
The unique LMS Black 5 No 4767 *George Stephenson* receives help from the fireman's shovel to lift the 'Cumbrian Mountain Express' up the gradient at Clapham, with the Carnforth to Skipton leg. *(Peter Millar)*
Mamiya 645, 150mm   Ektachrome 64   f4/5.6, 1/500

43

Steam in the Highlands
As in the good old days of Black Fives on the Highland line, No 5025 levels off after topping Drumochter Summit with the southbound working of the 'Speyside Express' on 20 July, 1981. British Rail chartered the newly retubed LMS Black Five from the Strathspey Railway where at its Aviemore depot it was possible to turn the locomotive for the return run back to Perth. *(Peter Lockley)*
Fujica ST605, 50mm   Agfa CT18   f5.6, 1/250

Late snowfall
Snow drifts against characteristic stone walls leading to Dent Head viaduct, where Stanier Black Five No 5305 threads the wild fells of the Yorkshire Dales with the southbound 'Cumbrian Mountain Express' on 22 March 1980. (*John Cooper-Smith*)
Mamiya 645   Ektachrome pro 64   f5.6/8, 1/250

Bahamas
Unique double chimneyed Jubilee No 5596 *Bahamas*, looking superb in LMS red livery, pulls away smartly from Chinley on 17 June, 1973 with an enthusiasts' special which travelled along the Hope Valley line. *Bahamas* hauled several special trains up and down the country in the early seventies before spending a long period out of action at the Dinting Railway Centre, Glossop. *(Michael Squire)*
Pentax SV 50mm   Kodachrome K11   f2.8/4, 1/250

Maroon meteor
Leander streaks through the barren landscape of the Yorkshire Dales on the legendary Settle and Carlisle line on 26 April, 1980. LMS No 5690, which is working the 'Leander Enterprise' special has just left Blea Moor tunnel and is crossing Dent Head viaduct. *(Peter J.C. Skelton)*
Contax RTS, 50mm   Kodachrome K64   f5.6, 1/250

Post-war black

Scots Guardsman was cleared by BR to work only two main line excursions during 1978, and here No 6115 makes for Cowburn tunnel with the 'Yorkshire Venturer'. A unique event took place on 11 November, 1978 when this train continued over the York circular route behind No 35028 *Clan Line* and crossed No 4771 *Green Arrow* hauling 'The Yorkshire Ranger'. *(Peter Lockley)*

Fujica ST 605, 50mm   Agfa CT18   f5.6, 1/250

Making up time
Having lost one hour behind modern traction en route from Crewe to Shrewsbury on 14 February, 1981, the 'Welsh Marches Express' now finds itself in the very capable hands of Stanier Pacific No 6201 *Princess Elizabeth*. After a photo-stop at Church Stretton the *Princess* storms away with maximum effort, leaving well behind the many photographers chasing in their cars. *(Peter Millar)*
Mamiya 645, 150mm   Ektachrome 64   f5.6, 1/500.

Shades of Shap

The maroon liveried No 46229 *Duchess of Hamilton* blends in well with the autumn colours as she masters the climb away from Baron Wood tunnels with a southbound 'Cumbrian Mountain Pullman' on 31 October, 1981. Although her assignment is a far cry from the heavy Anglo-Scottish trains she once hauled over the nearby Shap line, the S & C route is nevertheless a taxing one and the *Duchess* has her work cut out on this occasion. *(Michael Squire)*

Pentax K1000, 75mm zoom   *Fujichrome RD100*   *f5.6, 1/250*

Redcoat

The ever popular No 46229 *Duchess of Hamilton* feels at home in the Yorkshire fells as she tackles the stiff climb up to Ais Gill with a thirteen coach 'Cumbrian Mountain Pullman', shown here passing Horton in Ribblesdale on 24 October, 1981. The *Duchess* left York's National Railway Museum earlier in the day with three special dining coaches which were joined onto SLOA's Pullman set at Hellifield for the long drag up to Carlisle. (*Peter J.C.Skelton*)
Hasselblad 500CM, 150mm   Agfachrome pro R100S.   f5.6, 1/250

Where there's smoke
The SVR has two Ivatt 2MT Moguls, one of which is the lined green No 46521, formerly allocated to Oswestry for working on the Cambrian lines. The 2-6-0 puts on a spectacular smoke show as it leaves Knowlesands tunnel on 18 August, 1974. *(Martin Wilkins)*
Canon EF, 50mm   Kodachrome K25   f4, 1/250

Tractive effort

Two 2-8-0 freight locomotives consolidate their efforts and make short work of the stiff climb up to Oxenhope on the KWVR on 6 December, 1975. Making headway towards a strong morning sun are Stanier 8F No 8431 piloting ex-Swedish State Railways 'WD' No 1931 with a special train for the Wirral Railway Circle out of Keighley. (John S. Whiteley)

Pentax, 55mm　　　Kodachrome K11　　　f2.8/4, 1/250

In disguise
Storm clouds threaten over Keighley town as Barton-Wright's L & Y 0-6-0 No 52044 rushes out of the station and into the sun with a train for Oxenhope.

The 1887 engine is masquerading in a new livery during the filming of *The Railway Children* on 26 June 1971. (*L.A.Nixon*)
Leica M2, 50mm   Kodachrome K11

Echoes of Evercreech
Derby-built 2-8-0 No 13809, ex-Somerset and Dorset stalwart lovingly restored to appear in the Rainhill Rocket 150 celebrations, now has the chance to stretch its legs on main line duty as the engine passes Edale in charge of the 'Wyvern Express' on 31 October, 1981. Shortly after this picture was taken the '7F' had a brush with a low bridge near Belle Vue, Manchester, losing its chimney's rim. (Peter Millar)
Mamiya 645, 80mm   Ektachrome 64   f5.6, 1/250

Singled out

Victorian elegance returns in December 1981 with the first public steaming since 1938 of Patrick Stirling's Great Northern Railway 4-2-2 No 1. The enterprising Great Central Railway, through the courtesy of the NRM, York, paved the way for the 111-year old engine once again to turn those massive eight foot diameter driving wheels under its own steam. The winter's sun breaks out at Swithland's Sidings to highlight the scene as Driver John Bellwood masters the controls on 6 December 1981. (*Peter J.C.Skelton*)

Hasselblad 500CM, 80mm   *Ektachrome pro 64*   *f2.8/4, 1/500*

Waiting in the wings
Both preserved British 4-4-2 Atlantics are ex-Great Northern. Designed by Ivatt in 1898 the older of the two, No 990 *Henry Oakley* retired as long ago as 1937 after covering 1.2 million miles. This classic engine makes ready to pass the reviewing stands during the Rail 150 celebrations at Shildon on 31 August, 1975. *(Peter J.C.Skelton)*

Canon FTb, 50mm   *Kodachrome K64*   *f5.6/8, 1/125*

Gresley excellence
Heading 'The Salopian' from Carnforth to Shrewsbury, on 16 May, 1981 LNER A4 Pacific No 4498 *Sir Nigel Gresley* has plenty in reserve as the safety valves scream to herald its approach to the summit of Gresford bank. *(Peter J.C. Skelton)*

Contax RTS, 135mm   *Kodachrome K64*   *f4, 1/500*

Dairsie Mains
Still in its final BR livery of Brunswick passenger green, John Cameron's LNER streamlined A4 Pacific No 60009 *Union of South Africa* breathes out a pennant of pure steam just as winter approaches. The 'Streak' heads an enthusiasts' special on 29 November, 1980 near Dairsie Mains in its Scottish stamping ground. *(Peter Millar)*

Mamiya 645, 150mm   *Ektachrome pro 200*   *f4/5.6, 1/500*

Scotsman in flight

Withdrawn early in 1963, *Flying Scotsman* under the ownership of Alan Pegler was a popular engine for special trains until a year after the official end of steam on BR. Britain's oldest working standard gauge Pacific, No 4472 makes a fine sight as it draws towards Seascale station with the return 'Santa Steam' special on 30 December, 1978. *(Peter J.C.Skelton)*

Hasselblad 500CM, 80mm   *Agfachrome pro 50s*   *f2.8, 1/250*

Scotsman ascending
This view of LNER A3 Pacific No 4472 shows the engine hard at work tackling the bank at Giggleswick with the Skipton-Carnforth leg of a southbound 'Cumbrian Mountain Express' on 22 March 1980. *(Peter J. C. Skelton)*
Contax RTS, 50mm   Kodachrome K25   f2.8, 1/500

Aiming high
One of the first ex-LNER engines to benefit from BR's 'return to steam' programme, No 4771 *Green Arrow* picks up the sun on the northern approach to Birkett tunnel on 27 March, 1978 with the return working of the 'Norfolkman' special between Carlisle and Leeds. *(Martin Wilkins)*
Canon EF, 50mm   Kodachrome K25   f2.8, 1/500

Bold by night
No 4771 *Green Arrow*'s apple green livery contrasts with the maroon of newly restored No 46229 *Duchess of Hamilton* as both engines await the Rocket 150 cavalcade celebrations at Rainhill on 25 May, 1980. *(Peter J.C.Skelton)*
Contax RTS, 50mm   Kodachrome K25   f2/2.8, 30 secs

B1 by firelight
Instead of the passing cuttings being illuminated by No 1306 *Mayflower*'s firebox glow, the reverse can be seen during Guy Fawkes bonfire celebrations on the GCR at Loughborough, on 5 November, 1981. *(Graham Wignall)*
Mamiya 645, 80mm   Ektachrome 64

Double take
The 'Erlestoke Manor' Fund's charter train from Bristol to Pickering was the first revenue earning turn for LNER 2-6-0 class K1 No 2005 after its overhaul at Grosmont. The locomotive is seen piloting Lambton 0-6-2T No 5 at Green End on the scenic North Yorkshire Moors Railway on 8 June, 1974. The train was named 'The North Yorkshireman' but lost its headboard at York during a locomotive exchange en route to Grosmont. (*John Hunt*)

Pentax, 50mm   *Kodachrome K11*   *f4, 1/250*

Apple green
LNER 3-cylinder 4-4-0 No 246 *Morayshire* bursts out of a tree-lined embankment as it hauls the six coach 'Fair Maid' special away from Laurieston (Falkirk), and heads for Dundee over Scottish Region metals on 19 April, 1981. *(Peter Millar)*
Mamiya 645, 80mm   Ektachrome 64   f4/5.6, 1/250

Season's turn
Just as autumn's colours reach their best NER 'T2' No 2238, NELPG's 0-8-0 freight engine accelerates 'The North Eastern' train away from Levisham with a through working to Pickering from Grosmont (NYMR) on an enthusiasts' day during the 1976 season. (*John Hunt*)
Pentax, 50mm   Kodachrome K25   f2.8/4, 1/250

Rainhill marathon

After triumphantly tackling the continuous grades over the S & C route, NBR 0-6-0 finds the going easier at Settle Junction. En route from Falkirk to Bold Colliery for the Rocket 150 celebrations, *Maude* was the only engine to escape the Chief Fire Officer's decree. Nearly all other participants had to take a diesel pilot because of the fire risk during the very dry May spell in 1980. *(Peter J.C.Skelton)*

Contax RTS, 50mm   Kodachrome K25   f4, 1/250

Motive power depot
No 673 *Maude* simmers at the head of a distinguished line of locomotives and contributes to the smoke haze being illuminated by the Bold Colliery lights on 25 May, 1980. We may never again glance upon the spectacle of thirty steam locomotives breathing out a pall of smoke to recreate the atmosphere of a working steam shed. (*Peter J.C.Skelton*)
Contax RTS, 50mm   Kodachrome K25   f2/2.8, 30 secs

Light load
NELPG's P3 0-6-0 No 2392 looks far removed
from its BR days when as J27 No 65894 it
struggled up Seaton Bank through the North
East grime with a heavy coal train in tow. This
tree-top view shows the engine passing through
Thomasson Foss with a pick-up freight on the
panoramic North Yorkshire Moors line on 1
May, 1977. *(John Hunt)*
Pentax   Kodachrome K25
f2.8/4, 1/250

Great white plume
It is nearing the end of the summer's season as
GNR class J52 0-6-0ST No 1247 climbs slowly
towards Goathland on the NYMR on 28
August, 1976. This is a fine location for the
photographer, providing a combination of
horizontals, diagonals and curves. *(D.Fleming)*
Kodachrome

Winter's dream

Built after nationalisation to a Wordsell design of fifty years before, class J72 0-6-0T No 69023 *Joem* brings a winter season train over Mytholmes viaduct on the KWVR during February 1969. It was one of Newcastle's station pilots before withdrawal by BR. *(Mrs. D.A.Robinson)*

Kodak Retina 11c   *Ektachrome 64*   *f5.6, 1/250*

December sun
On 17 December, 1978 ex-LNER class N2 0-6-2T No 4744 rockets away from Rothley in the style with which it worked Great Northern suburban services out of Kings Cross. *(Peter Lockley)*
Fujica ST605, 50mm   Agfa CT18   f5.6, 1/250

Britannia Continental

Having been fitted with air brake apparatus on the Nene Valley Railway, BR Standard 7P6F Pacific No 70000 is now equipped to haul Continental rolling stock.

Britannia can be seen climbing away from Lynch Bridge on 6 December, 1980 with such a set, forming the 'Santa Express' during a crisp sunny day. *(Laurie Manns) Bronica S2A, 75mm*   *Ektachrome pro 64*   *f4/5.6, 1/500*

City of Peterborough
BR Standard class 5 No 73050 *City of Peterborough* looks immaculate after complete overhaul by local engineering firm Peter Brotherhood Ltd. The ex-Somerset and Dorset locomotive heads a Nene Valley train on 23 August, 1981 over gradients more gentle than those of the Mendip hills. *(Graham Wignall)*
Mamiya 645, 80mm   *Ektachrome 64*

Brunswick green

In ex-works condition, Standard class '4' No 75027 prepares to leave Sheffield Park for Horsted Keynes on the Bluebell Railway, 31 August, 1980. Allocated for most of its career to the Western Region, this engine hauled trains on the Somerset & Dorset line before ending its BR days in the Carnforth area. *(Nils Huxtable)*
Pentax K1000, 50mm   Kodachrome K64

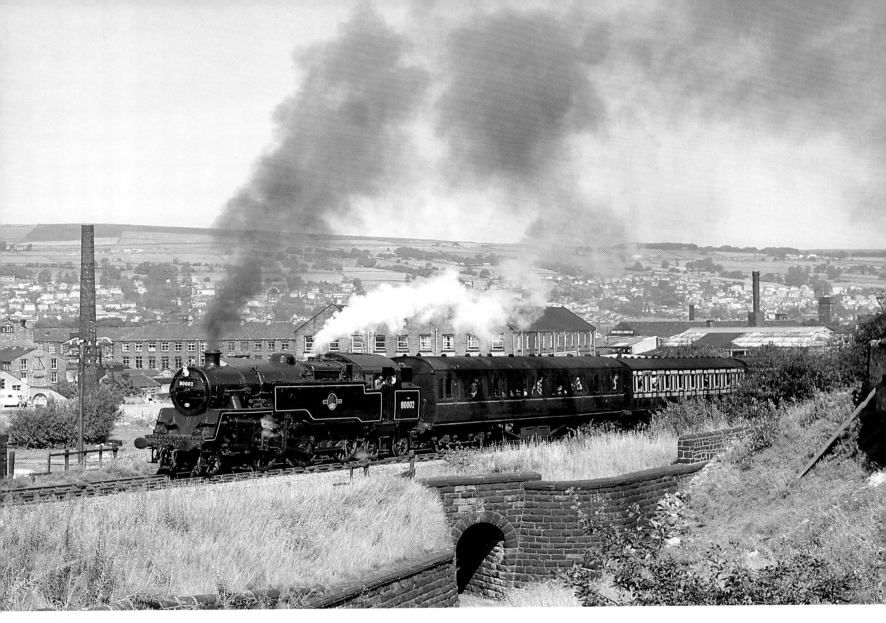

Early days
Nine class 4MT 2-6-4T locomotives have been saved from the cutter's torch. The first of these Riddles designed engines to be restored to working order, No 80002, spent the final years of its career as a banker at Beattock. It is shown here on 5 September, 1971 leaving Keighley with the climb to Oxenhope ahead. (*John S.Whiteley*)
Minolta, 55mm   Kodachrome K11   f4, 1/250

New livery
Although the correct paint scheme for the 4MT 2-6-4Ts is BR lined black, No 80135 looks quite acceptable in passenger green livery. The engine is passing Moorgates with a southbound train for Pickering during a gala weekend on the NYMR in September 1980. *(Keith Glover)*

Nikon EM   Kodachrome K64   f5.6, auto

Gordon the big blue engine
Several WD 2-10-0s survive today in Greece. No 600 *Gordon* remained an Army engine on the Longmoor Military Railway until a safe home was found on the SVR.

The 'Austerity' 2-10-0 crosses Victoria bridge with a Bridgnorth to Bewdley train on a lovely spring day in April, 1976. *(Hugh Ballantyne)*
Leica M3, 50mm   Kodachrome K25   f2/2.8, 1/250

Artistic licence

Rare outing over Southern Region's metals for David Shepherd's 2-10-0 class 9F No 92203 *Black Prince*. The famous artist leans out of the cab absorbing the exhilarating atmosphere of a powerful steam locomotive in full flight as his pride accelerates away from Romsey on 20 April, 1975. The locomotive is now kept at the East Somerset Railway at Cranmore. *(Michael Squire)*

Pentax SV, 50mm   Kodachrome K11   f4, 1/250

Sunspot
The sun breaks through the clouds to highlight the arches of Battymoss viaduct, Ribblehead on 30 September, 1978. No 92220 *Evening Star*, the last steam locomotive to be built for BR in 1960, is a suitable choice for the 'Bishop Treacy' commemorative train. *(Peter J.C. Skelton)*
Olympus OM1, 50mm   *Kodachrome K64*   *f5.6, 1/250*

In name and spirit
Only top hats and tails are needed to complete this apparently Dickensian scene. *Lion*, built for the Liverpool and Manchester Railway in 1838, takes part in braking trials between Southport and Burscough Bridge on 12 May, 1980 prior to revisiting haunts of its youth in the Rainhill celebrations. *(John S. Whiteley)*

Pentax, 85mm   Kodachrome K25   f4, 1/250

Metropolitan red
The attractive livery of 0-6-0PT No L89, turned out on the KWVR in London Transport colours, blends in well with the scene at Damens Loop. The departure shows the engine's dislike for the type of coal being used as it builds up its fire for the run up to Oxenhope, May 1975. *(John S. Whiteley)*
Pentax, 55mm   Kodachrome K11   f4, 1/250

Lending a hand

Cambria, a Hunslet Austerity 0-6-0ST built in 1953, pilots Fairburn 2-6-4T No 2085 on the Lakeside Railway on 31 May, 1975. The pair make an impressive exit out of Haverthwaite tunnel with a LCGB special and make for the Lakeside terminal with its panoramic view across Lake Windermere to the magnificent peaks of the Lake District. *(Peter J.C. Skelton)*

Canon FTb, 50mm   *Kodachrome K64*   *f4, 1/250*

Cavalcade
To commemorate the centenary of A1X 0-6-0T No 10 *Sutton*, the Kent & East Sussex Railway staged a cavalcade on 26 September, 1976 to show their impressive stud of locomotives. Right to left are: 0-6-0ST No 23, Norwegian 2-6-0 No 19,

0-6-0ST No 17 *Arthur*, 0-4-0T No 12, A1X 0-6-0T No 10 *Sutton*, 0-6-0ST No 23, ex-LMR 0-6-0ST No 196 *Errol Lonsdale*, A1X 0-6-0T No 3 *Bodiam* and propping up the rear 0-6-0ST No 26. *(Michael Squire)*
Canon EX, 50mm   Kodachrome K25   f4, 1/250

Study in stone and steam
The Lambton tank crosses two bridges and a stream at Water Arc on the NYMR with a Grosmont-Goathland train on 1 May, 1977. Before preservation the 0-6-2T No 29 tackled far tougher assignments for the NCB at Philadelphia, Co Durham.
(Peter Lockley)
Fujica ST605, 50mm   *Agfa CT18*   *f5.6/8, 1/250*

Pocket-size *Lord Mayor*
In steam for the first time in eight years, 1893-built Hudswell Clark 0-4-0ST *Lord Mayor* shuffles away from Keighley on 18 July, 1891 with a test train, comprising a teak bodied six-wheeled brake of 1888. The locomotive's previous owner was a scrap dealer, Messrs George Cohen. *(Graham Lockley)*
Fujica ST605, 50mm   Agfa CT18   f4/5.6, 1/250

Smoke and shadow
In 1973 the SVR only ran trains between Bridgnorth and Hampton Loade. The sun of mid-winter catches the exhaust in the crisp cold air from ex-LMR 'Austerity'

No 193 as it passes Eardington with a post-Christmas train on 30 December, 1973. *(Hugh Ballantyne)*
Leica M3, 50mm   Kodachrome K11   f2 8/4, 1/500

Five foot three
Classic ex-Great Northern Railway (Ireland) inside cylinder 4-4-0 class S No 171 *Slieve Gullion* bursts into a deep cutting near Castleton with the Railway Preservation Society of Ireland's steam special on the Dublin to Mullingar main line. Although the Society's headquarters are at Whitehead in Northern Ireland, weekend tours take place over the Coras Iompair Eirann lines also. (*Michael Squire*)
Canon EX, 50mm   Kodachrome K25   f4, 1/250

Silver Mines Railtour
Working hard against strong crosswinds at the head of the RPSI Silver Mines Railtour on 29 September, 1974, between Nenagh and Roscrea is ex-LMS (NCC) class WT 2-6-4T No 4. This engine built in 1947 was one of the last steam locomotives to remain in service on the Northern Ireland Railways. It was finally withdrawn in 1970. *(Maurice Crowe)*
Practica Super TL, 50mm   *Agfa CT18*   *f5.6/8, 1/250*

Centenarian
Despite its size and age ex-Great Southern & Western Railway 0-6-0 class J15
No 186 still manages a brisk pace as it approaches Sligo with a modest train forming
the RPSI special on the CIE main line from Dublin. *(Michael Squire)*
Canon EX, 50mm   Kodachrome K25   f4, 1/250

Great little train
Just a pleasant scene on the only 2′ 6″ gauge railway in Wales – the Welshpool and Llanfair Railway. No 1 *Earl* is one of two Beyer Peacock 0-6-0T locomotives built for the opening of the line back in 1902, and is pictured on 8 April, 1977 hauling a set of Austrian coaches through the charming countryside. *(Hugh Ballantyne)*
Leica M3, 50mm   Kodachrome K25

Welsh Prince
One of the oldest operating engines in the UK is this 0-4-0ST built by George England & Co in 1863. No 2 *Prince*, as strong as ever after a recent overhaul, heads one of the intensive service trains for holiday makers on the very picturesque Festinoig Railway, and passes through a rock cutting after emerging from the 'new' tunnel at Moelwyn. *(Hugh Ballantyne)*
Leica M4-2, 50mm   Kodachrome K25

Grand old gent
Bursting into the sunshine out of the shading trees, trundles beautifully restored No 3, an ex-Corris Railway 0-4-2ST, built by the Hughes Loco & Tramway Engine Works at Loughborough in 1878. Now in the loving care of the 2′ 3″ gauge Talyllyn Railway *Sir Haydn* is in charge of the 11.50 train from Towyn Wharf and passes through this attractive setting out of Brynglas, heading up the valley towards Abergynolwyn and Nant Gwernol. *(Hugh Ballantyne)*

Leica M4-2, 50mm   *Kodachrome K25*   *f2.8/4, 1/250*

Water stop
As can be seen on the 1′ 11½″ gauge tracks out of Aberystwyth, British Rail never did dispense with steam entirely. Vale of Rheidol 2-6-2T No 8 *Llywelyn* in rail blue livery, attracts the attention of two young admirers as the engine pauses for refreshment at Devils Bridge. *(Peter J.C.Skelton)*

Contax RTS, 50mm   *Kodachrome K64*   *f2.8, 1/125*

Manx marvel
An unspoilt scene at Douglas Station with beautiful Beyer Peacock-built 2-4-0T No 13 *Kissack* making a spirited departure. Passengers on the Isle of Man 3' 0" gauge railway can expect a delightful run on the 15½ mile trip to Port Erin. (*L.A.Nixon*)
Leica M2, 50mm   *Kodachrome K11*